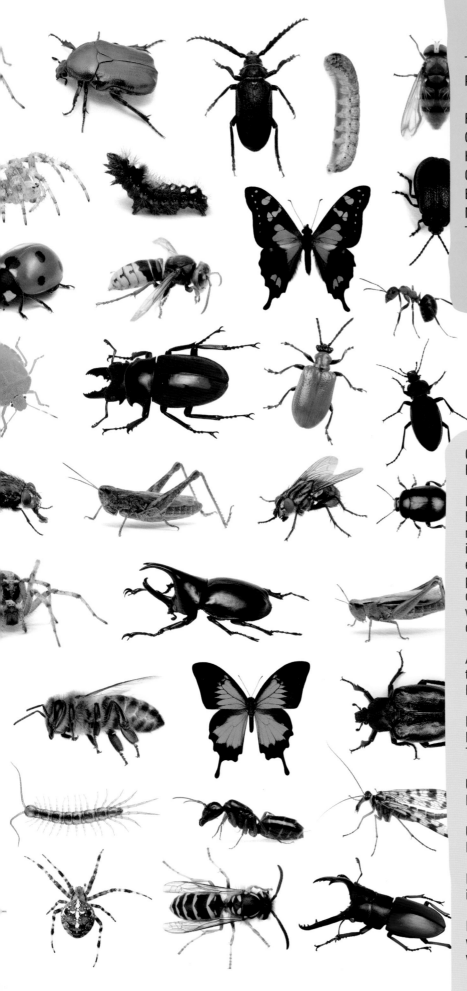

Thanks to
Perfect Bound Ltd

First published in
Great Britain in 2019 by
Hungry Tomato Ltd
Old Bakery Studios
Blewetts Wharf
Malpas Road, Truro
TR1 1JQ, UK

Copyright 2020
Hungry Tomato Ltd

A CIP catalogue record for
this book is available from the
British Library

Beetle Books and Hungry
Banana are imprints of Hungry
Tomato Ltd

US Edition (Beetle Books)
ISBN 978-1-913077-23-5

UK Edition (Hungry Banana)
ISBN 978-1-913077-30-3

Printed and bound
in China

Discover more at
www.mybeetlebooks.com
www.hungrytomato.com

102 THINGS

TO DO...

PAUL MASON

CONTENTS

Top tips and fun facts

With LOTS of new things to do, you'll never be bored again. Here are some useful tips and facts to help you have fun, stay safe, and make good friends.

YOU NEED SUNLIGHT

Too much sunlight is harmful, but everyone needs some. Sunshine causes your body to produce vitamin D, which helps you get chemicals called calcium and phosphate from food. These make bones, teeth, and muscles grow strong.

BEING OUTSIDE MIGHT MAKE YOU SEE BETTER

One scientific report says that for every hour you play outside, you are 2 per cent less likely to need glasses.

SAFETY OUTSIDE

Part of the fun of being outside can be getting away from adults. This is fine—as long as your adults:

- know where you are
- have said it's OK

RAINY-DAY GEAR

An umbrella will keep you mostly dry on a rainy day, if there is no wind. For full protection, though, you need:

- Waterproof hat, coat, and pants
- Rubber boots

BE TRUSTWORTHY

If your friend tells you something they don't want everyone to know, do not rush off and tell someone else. And remember, friends never say bad things about each other to other people.

SAFETY IN NUMBERS

If you are going out to do some good work for your neighborhood, take a friend. It's safer and whatever job you do will take half as long!

BUILDING YOUR COMMUNITY

If you and your neighbors do things for each other, you get to know them. You might even become friends. Knowing the people who live around you makes life more interesting.

HELPING THOSE WHO CAN'T HELP THEMSELVES

Some of your neighbors might not be able to do things for themselves. For example, someone elderly could find it tricky to reach up and clean their windows. A neighbor who is out at work all day may not be able to walk their dog. A new kid in the neighborhood might not know the way to school yet.

SPEAK AND LISTEN

It is important to listen to your friends, rather than just always saying what you think. Don't worry—if they are good at listening as well, you will get your chance to talk.

BEING ACTIVE MAKES YOU SMARTER

Being outside usually means you are being active. You might decide to go for a hike, build a shelter, or go on a hunt to photograph wildlife, for example.

Several investigations have shown that students who get physically fit usually start to get better grades:

- Their memories improve
- Their brains start to make connections in new ways
- They can concentrate better

STAY SAFE!

If you are ever going into the house of someone you do not know well, make sure one of your parents knows where you are going and has said it's OK. The first time you call on someone new, it would be a good idea to take one of your parents with you.

1. Sleep out

Sleeping out with your friends is a great adventure. Plan ahead (and check the weather forecast) and you will still be talking about the sleep-out years later.

THINGS YOU DEFINITELY NEED:

- Sleeping mat
- Sleeping bag
- A drink
- A light

THINGS YOU MIGHT LIKE:

- A warm, dry night
- Food
- Bug spray
- Pillow
- Tent

1 Pick a place. Your sleep-out site needs to be somewhere level, which you can easily reach, and which is safe. Lots of kids do their first sleep-out in a back yard.*

2 Clear the ground. Decide exactly where you are going to sleep. Check the ground for stones, sticks, and anything else that might keep you awake.

3 Enjoy being outdoors. Just because there's no TV or internet doesn't mean there is nothing to do except go to sleep.

4 Get some rest. When everyone's tired, climb into your sleeping bags and (if you didn't bring one and are using a folded-up coat instead) wish you had a pillow. Don't worry, though: you will get to sleep.

5 Do a clean-up. Everyone will probably wake up as soon as it gets light. Check the sleep-out site for trash—if there is any, pick it up to take away.

If you are sleeping in a tent, make sure there is nothing sharp that could stick up through the floor.

Stick together—but don't put your sleep mat TOO close to other people in case they snore!

SLEEP-OUT SAFETY

Always check everyone's parents think the place you have picked is safe for sleeping out. Make sure you have permission to sleep there, too.

*Make a pact not to chicken out later and go indoors!

2. Build a campfire

TOP TIP: make sure there's room to get a match to the kindling!

Campfires are great for talking around, toasting food, and keeping warm, so knowing how to make one is a useful skill.

1 **Find a fire site.** Your fire needs to be at least 6½ feet (2 meters) from anything that could catch light. Build a ring of big rocks to stop the fire spreading.

2 **Build a fire teepee.** In the middle goes the kindling: dry leaves and grass, which catch fire easily. Then add the twigs, and a few larger sticks.

3 **Light the fire.** Light the kindling. If you light one edge and blow on it, the flame should spread—but don't stay close for too long.

FIRE SAFETY
- Never build a campfire if there is a fire ban, or where there is a risk of wildfires.
- Don't try and start a fire without an adult present, and always ask a parent for permission first.

ALL YOU NEED
- Big rocks
- Dry leaves, grass, twigs, larger sticks, and small logs
- Matches

The ring should be about 20 inches (half a meter) across.

3. Find Orion

Orion is one of the most famous star constellations. It can be seen in the night sky from anywhere in the world.

1 **Look for Orion's belt.** Orion the Hunter's belt is made of three bright stars in a line, close together.

2 **Find his shoulders and knees.** Above and below Orion's belt (but farther apart), look for four more bright stars.

3 **Look for Orion's sword.** Between Orion's belt and knees are three more stars, close together. In the middle is the Orion Nebula, a place where stars are born.

4 **Find the rest of Orion.** Now you have the basic shape, you can pick out the rest of the stars that make Orion and his bow.

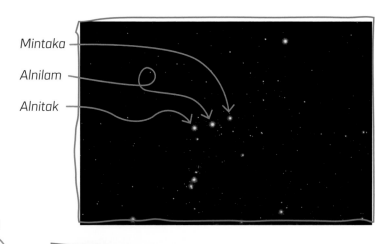

Mintaka
Alnilam
Alnitak

Shoulders
Betelgeuse

Bellatrix

Knees
Saiph

Rigel

4. Go on a hike

Going on a hike means walking somewhere—usually to a place farther away than you would normally walk.

1 **Pick a route.** Decide where to go. Short hikes, 2½–3 miles (4–5 km), are good to start with.

2 **Work out your timing.** Most people can walk at about 3–3¾ mph (5–6 kph), so a 6¼ mile (10 km) hike will take 2–3 hours, including stops. Take water to drink, and on hikes of more than 2 hours, take food too.

3 **Gather your gear.** Check the weather forecast and decide whether to put rain gear, warm clothes, sunscreen, etc. in your backpack.

4 **Go hiking.** Stick to your route, stop when you are tired or see something interesting, and enjoy being outside!

ALL YOU NEED
- Friends
- Comfortable shoes
- Backpack
- Drink and food

ROUTE NOTES
Tell an adult your route and when you will be back. Then they will know if you're late and where to look for you.

5. Go on a plastic raid

Plastic trash can stay around for years. It looks bad, and harms animals and plants. Help your beach or park become plastic-free!

ALL YOU NEED

- Volunteers
- Trash bags
- Gloves to protect your hands

1 **Advertize!** Tell your friends, the school council, and your local newspaper the time and date of the plastic raid.

2 **Organize teams.** Have someone responsible in charge of teams of three. Each team picks up all the plastic in its area.

ADVANCE PLANNING

Check with the local council or beach owner to check:
a) that your raid is allowed
a) what you should do with the plastic

3 **Sort the plastic.** Each team uses two trash bags each, for recyclable and non-recyclable plastic.

4 **Tidy up.** Recycle what you can, and dump the rest of the waste in the trash.

Maybe you could organize cakes and drinks for the volunteers?

6. Play outdoor Furious Birds

This is a great game for people of any age—as long as they aren't scared of a bit of water.

1 **Fill the balloons**. Draw furious bird faces on the balloons, fill them with water, and put them in the bucket.

2 **Chalk up some pigs.** Chalk out some pig faces on the ground.
   Big pig faces = 1 point
   Smaller faces = 2 points
   Tiny faces = 3 points

3 **Attack.** From behind a chalk line, take turns to throw water balloons at the pigs. If you wipe one out, you get the points.

4 **Clean up.** Once all the pigs are gone, pick up the burst balloons and brush away any leftover chalk.

ALL YOU NEED
- Wash-away chalk
- Water balloons
- Marker pen
- Bucket

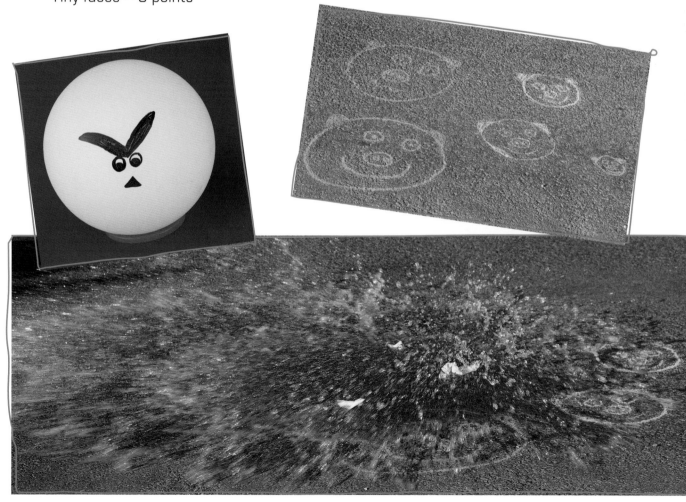

7. Take your friends on a treasure hunt

ALL YOU NEED
- A compass
- A notepad and pencil
- White paper and colored pens
- Old coffee or tea leaves
- Treasure

This activity is in two parts. First, you make a treasure map for your friends to follow. Then you hide the treasure and they try to find it.

1 Find a hiding place. Find somewhere to hide the treasure. It could be under some bushes, up a tree, or buried in a hole.

2 Work out a route. Now work out a route from there to the starting place. It should be as confusing as possible! Go around buildings and over obstacles.

3 Count it out. Retrace your route back to the treasure spot. Count the direction and number of steps from one stop to another. Note everything on the notepad.

4 Draw the map. Draw out the route carefully, in pencil at first. Add directions like: "Walk 15 steps due east." or "After 21 steps, turn north between two trees."

5 Make the map look old. Rub the map with old coffee or tea, then leave it to dry in the sun. Rip the edges and scrunch it up.

6 Hide your treasure. Your treasure chest could be a tin containing some cakes, a candy bar, or a sandwich for lunch. Don't make it anything too valuable, in case someone else finds it!

7 Set your friends the treasure-hunt challenge. They could do it together, or one at a time (in which case the person who finds the treasure in the least time wins it).

8. Go on a bug safari

You don't have to go to Africa to go on safari—not if it's a bug safari. A backyard or park is all that's required.

1 **Draw a grid.** Name the things you expect to find (and you could draw them too). Leave space for unexpected bugs!

2 **Start hunting.** Now start looking for bugs. Some might be flying. Others will be under rocks, on leaves, or beneath bushes.

3 **Add it all up.** Add up what you find. Are some bugs more common than others? What size are they? Why might there be more of these?

Every time you see a bug, add a mark to your grid. You could take a photo, too.

9. Organize a night hike

At night, outdoor smells and noises are different. Familiar routes no longer look the same.

1 **Set a meeting place.** Tell everyone where to meet and when. As they arrive, put their names on a list.

2 **Stick together.** On the hike, make sure the group doesn't get separated. One person leads the way. Someone else goes at the back and calls out if the leaders get too far ahead.

3 **Stop and listen.** Once in a while, stop, turn off your flashlights and listen. Everything sounds louder (and more creepy!) in the dark.

4 **Check everyone back in.** When you get back, tick off people's names on the list to make sure no one has been left behind.

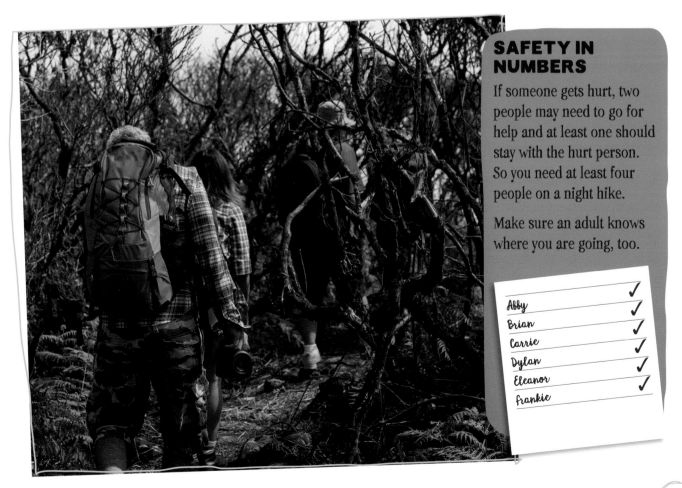

SAFETY IN NUMBERS

If someone gets hurt, two people may need to go for help and at least one should stay with the hurt person. So you need at least four people on a night hike.

Make sure an adult knows where you are going, too.

Abby ✓
Brian ✓
Carrie ✓
Dylan ✓
Eleanor ✓
Frankie

10. Fix a puncture

Imagine: you're going out for a ride with your friends in an hour, but when you get to your bike—argh! Flat tire! Here's what to do:

1 **Remove the wheel.** Many bikes have a quick-release lever for this, but you might need to use a wrench.

2 **Remove one side of the tire.** Use your tire levers to lift one side of the tire off the wheel. The first bit is tricky, then it gets easier.

3 **Lift off the other side.** Repeat the process, but lever the other side of the tire off on the SAME side of the wheel as before.
You have now removed the tire and the inner tube inside it.

4 **Find the puncture.** Pull the inner tube out of the tire. Pump up the inner tube and you'll hear a little hiss of air where the puncture is and can mark with the chalk.

5 **Check the tire.** Check the tire to see if a thorn or sharp rock is sticking through anywhere. If it is, take it out, or the inner tube will get another puncture.

6 **Patch the puncture.** Use the sandpaper to roughen the tube and then stick the repair patch carefully over the puncture. Press down hard, then add a little air to the tube: just enough to make it round.

7 **Tuck in the inner tube.** Put the inner tube back inside the tire.

8 **Put the tire back on the wheel.** Start by putting the valve through the valve hole. Then push one side of the tire into place over the edge of the wheel. Slowly work around—you might need to use the levers for the last bit.

9 **Check the tube and finish.** Make sure the tube is properly inside the tire. If it is, push the other side of the tire onto the wheel.
You might have to use your tire levers for the last bit.

10 **Pump up and go!** Pump up the tire as hard as you can, which will help keep the patch in place. Put the wheel back on your bike, and go and meet your friends.

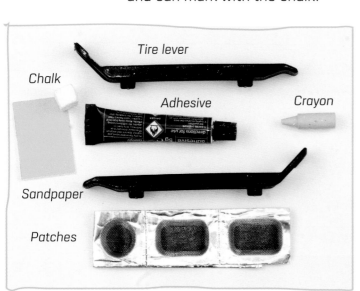

Tire lever

Chalk

Adhesive

Crayon

Sandpaper

Patches

①

Unscrew the valve
to pump air into
the tube

②

③

④

⑥

⑧

HINSON

11. Learn to yodel

A yodel is a loud sound using the natural break between your normal voice and a high-pitched version of it.

1 **Find the yodel break.** Start singing "Ohhhhhhh" as low as you can. Keep getting higher until you hear the break.

2 **Practice.** Keep going back and forth between the two versions of your voice. You can use different sounds, not only "Ohhhhhhh."

3 **Sing a yodel!** Most yodels use one low note and two high ones. Try out the cowboy yodel:
   "Yodel ay (low)*, ee* (high) *dee* (high)."

Yodelling was originally used in the Alps to communicate across the mountains. It eventually became popular with cowboy singers.

12. Play "She'll be Comin' Round the Mountain"
on a ukulele

1 **Learn these chords**. You can play "She'll be comin' round the Mountain" with five simple chords. To play the chords, run your thumb down the strings from top to bottom. This is called strumming.

Maybe on your sleep-out [see page 10] you'd like to sing a few songs? Here is a simple one to practice on the ukulele before you go.

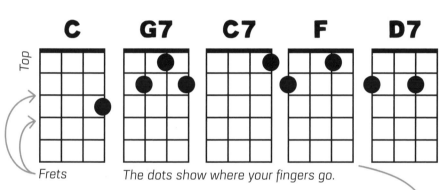

Top

C   **G7**   **C7**   **F**   **D7**

Frets   *The dots show where your fingers go.*

2 **Add the chords to the song**. At first, just play the chords when the song says. When you get more confident, you can add some extra strums.

ALL YOU NEED

- A ukulele (really, that's it)

Chorus

      C
She'll be comin' round the mountain

when she comes

She'll be comin' round the mountain
      G7
when she comes
      C   C7
She'll be comin' round the mountain,
      F   D7
She'll be comin' round the mountain
      C   G7
She'll be comin' round the mountain
      C
when she comes

Verse

  She'll be driving six white horses when she comes
  She'll be driving six white horses when she comes
  She'll be driving six white horses,
  She'll be driving six white horses
  She'll be driving six white horses when she comes.

13. Paint like Pollock

ALL YOU NEED

- Big bit of paper
- Big sheets of cardboard
- Paints with different colors
- One paintbrush per color

Jackson Pollock is a famous artist. He uses splashes and drops of color to make bright, many-layered paintings.

1 **Lay out your paper.** Put it on the ground, right in the middle of the big bits of cardboard.

2 **Add one color.** Load up your brush, then flick the paint onto the paper.* Different heights and strengths of flick will give different effects.

3 **Add more colors.** Keep adding colors until the painting looks just right to you.

* Make sure you are wearing scruffy, old clothes

14. Make a rock-stack sculpture

These sculptures look great anywhere—what's really fun is to build one, then leave it for other people to enjoy.

1 **Find some rocks.** Flat rocks are usually best. You will need a mixture of sizes.

2 **Work out how they fit together.** The biggest rocks usually go at the bottom.

3 **Check each layer for balance.** Make sure each layer is solidly balanced on the one underneath. You don't want your sculpture to blow over in the wind!

ALL YOU NEED
- Different-sized rocks
- Patience

15. Make a pine-cone bird feeder

A bird feeder is a sure way to attract birds. In winter, it might even help them stay alive.

ALL YOU NEED

- Pine or fir cones (dried out so they don't open)
- Lard
- Bird seed
- Raisins
- Peanuts
- Grated cheese
- A mixing bowl
- Scissors
- String

1 **Mix it up.** Chop the lard into small pieces and mix with the other ingredients. Use your fingers to squish it all together.

2 **Make a cone ball.** Put three or four pine cones together and bind them up with string. Leave about 20 inches (50 cm) of string dangling.

3 **Add the food.** Press the food on to the cone ball, covering it completely.

4 **Hang the feeder.** Tie the loose end of the string to a branch or fence. Hungry birds will soon start to arrive.

16. Photograph birds

Now that you have a bird feeder (see page 26) you have a great chance to become a wildlife photographer.

1 **Line up your shot.** Decide the best angle to take the photo from. Avoid looking towards the sun.

2 **Hide yourself.** Hide in a nearby building if there is one. If not, maybe you could put up a tent, or build yourself a shelter like the one on page 28.

3 **Be patient.** Try to keep still as you wait for the birds to arrive. They will not approach if you are wriggling about or making a noise.

MAKE A NATURE ALBUM

Once you have photos of different birds, you could put together a nature notebook with facts about what you have seen.

1 Research your birds. First, you need to know which birds you photographed. Find out by asking people, looking in books in the library, and researching on the internet.

2 Add some facts. Now organize what you know. Each photograph might have an entry like this:

> Name: Robin
> Male/female
> When photographed:
> May 2020
> Place: San Diego,
> California
> Behavior: fast-moving,
> gathering bugs (to feed
> chicks?)

3 Put together an album. You could do this by printing everything and sticking it down in a notebook. Or you could make an online album.

17. Build a forest shelter

Whether you are outside in the day or sleeping out at night, a shelter comes in handy. It can shield you from rain, wind, and hot sunshine.

ALL YOU NEED

- Two trees close together
- One long, straight, fallen branch
- Lots of thick sticks
- Two 10-foot (3-m) lengths of rope or strong cord
- Branches with leaves on

PERMISSION

If you are gathering wood for a shelter, make sure you have permission from the landowner:
a) to be on the land
b) to collect wood

1 **Assemble your branches.** The long branch should be a bit longer than the gap between the two trees. The thick sticks should be at least 5 feet (1.5 m) long.

2 **Tie on the long branch.** Tie the long branch to the trees, parallel to the ground, about 3 feet (1 m) up.

3 **Lay on the thick sticks.** Now lean the thick sticks against the long branch. The longer they are, the more space there will be under your shelter.

4 **Add leafy branches.** Try to find branches that have fallen but still have leaves. Lay these on the outer side of your "wall."

5 **Install a bed.** The last thing to do is make the shelter comfortable. Gather together soft, dry leaves and make a thick bed of them under the roof.

Ideally the sticks should be no more than 45° from the ground. An angle of 30° will give you more room, but you will need longer sticks.

30°
45°

If you can only find one tree in the right place, build a sloping shelter like this

WHICH DIRECTION?

If your shelter is to hide from wind and rain, find two trees that are across the direction the wind is coming from.

If your shelter is for shade, find trees linked by an imaginary east–west line. Your shelter will give most shade if it faces north (north of the Equator) or south (south of the Equator). You can find north using a watch with hands:

North of the Equator, turn the watch until the hour hand points directly at the Sun. Now imagine a line halfway between the 12 on the watch face and the hour hand. That line points south, so north is the opposite way.

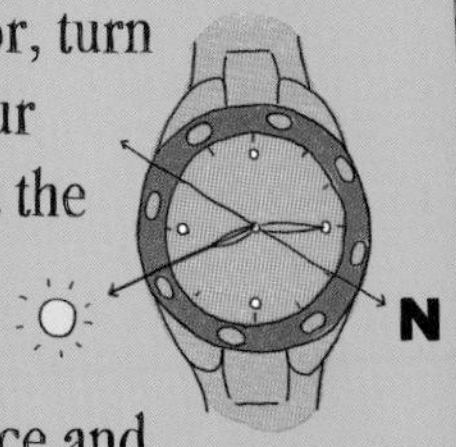

South of the Equator, point the 12 on the watch face at the Sun; north is halfway between the 12 and the hour hand.

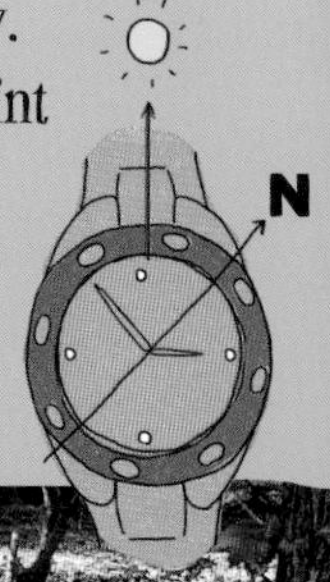

18. Go for a picnic

ALL YOU NEED

- Bread
- Cheese
- Tomatoes
- Salt and mayonnaise
- Something to drink
- Knife
- Picnic blanket

People often say food tastes better outdoors. Going for a simple picnic with your family or friends is a good way to find out.

1 **Pick a picnic spot.** Remember you have to carry your picnic stuff, so somewhere a long way off might not be ideal.

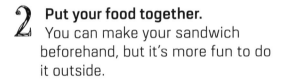

2 **Put your food together.** You can make your sandwich beforehand, but it's more fun to do it outside.

3 **Pack in, pack out.** Once the picnic is over, check your spot to make sure you have left no trash behind.

Lay slices of cheese, then tomato on the bread. Sprinkle on a teeny bit of salt, then a thin layer of mayonnaise.

19. Cook potatoes on a campfire

If you build a campfire (see page 11) and feel hungry, why not use the fire's heat to bake some potatoes?

1 **Preparation.** Prepare the potatoes by pricking the surface all over, then cutting them in half. Put butter and a tiny bit of salt in the middle, press the halves together and wrap them in aluminum foil.

2 **Place the potatoes.** Not right in the fire!

3 **Wait... then eat.** Normal potatoes take at least 45 minutes to cook. Sweet potatoes take half as long.

Rake some red-hot coals to the edge of the fire. Put the potatoes on them, then rake more coals over the top. Repeat as the coals cool down.

20. Go crabbing

Crabbing—catching crabs by dangling bait—is a fun way to spend time at the seaside.

ALL YOU NEED

- String or handline
- Bucket
- Small fishing net
- Old small mesh laundry bag
- Bait (crabs like fish)

1 **Prepare the bucket.** Put seawater in the bucket, plus seaweed and pebbles. This makes it more like the crab's normal surroundings.

2 **Bait up.** Put your bait inside the small mesh laundry bag and tie it to the string.

3 **Lower the bait.** Lower the bait into the water until you feel it touch the bottom.

4 **Pull up a crab.** When you feel a crab nibbling at the bait, lift it gently up and out of the water. Put the crab carefully into the bucket.

5 **Identify the crabs.** If you have different kinds of crab, see if you can identify the different species you've found.

6 **Release the crabs.** Once you've finished crabbing, carefully release the crabs back into the sea where they belong.

Try not to have too many crabs in a bucket: the crabs will not like it.

Wind a bit of line around your finger. This makes it easier to feel crabs pulling on it.

Northern Kelp Crab

Dungeness Crab

King Crab

Blue Crab

Fiddler Crab

Mitten Crab

CRAB CARE!

Be careful when picking up crabs: if they pinch, it is very hard to make them let go.

Hold the crab with your finger and thumb on either side of the shell, so you don't hurt the crab. Hold it behind its pincers, so it cannot reach you with them.

21–25. Five more things...

Here are five more things to do outdoors. For some of them you will need help from your parents. (Usually, help with paying.)

21 Learn to rock-climb
Many outdoor centers have rock-climbing courses lasting half a day or a day.

22 Go off-road cycling
Make sure to pick a trail that your bike can do. Don't try to ride along a rocky, bumpy path on a drop-bar road bike.

23 Try a junior run
In some places there are properly organized, timed runs around marked courses in parks and other open spaces. The courses may be 1¼–3 miles (2–5 km) long. Just get an adult to register you online, turn up, and run.

24 Set up a skateboard slalom
All you need is a safe area, chalk to mark the start and finish lines, a stopwatch, and some cones (or old drinks bottles with water inside).

25 Read a book
Find a quiet, comfortable spot (take cushions if you like...), settle down, and concentrate on your favorite book for a while.

26. Make money from old things

ALL YOU NEED:

- Pen and notepad
- Something to take digital photos (possibly)

A rainy day is a good opportunity to start earning some money, by selling your old things.

1 **Have a clear-out.** Decide what you are going to target: old clothes, toys, books, or sports equipment, perhaps. Get everything out and decide what to sell. If you haven't used something for a year, do you still need it?

2 **Work out your prices.** Make a list of your prices. If something is rare or very popular (e.g. a first edition of the first-ever Harry Potter book) it might be worth a lot. If it is in poor condition it will be worth less.

Type of item:	Good-condition value
Sports equipment	30% of new cost
Books	10–15% of new cost
Clothes	10% of new cost
Toys	10% of new cost

You could sell your items in a yard sale. Or maybe you could ask a teacher to organize a market at school?

STAY SAFE

If you are planning to sell your things online, ask an adult to post the ad for you. If you want to sell your stuff at a yard or garage sale, make sure an adult knows what you are doing and comes along if they think it is necessary.

27. Write your pet's life story

ALL YOU NEED

- Pen and paper, or a computer and printer
- Library or internet access

If you have no pets, don't worry: it's even more fun writing about an imaginary pet. How about a pet crocodile, honey badger, or pterodactyl?

1 **Research your pet.** Find out a bit about your pet. If it's a dachshund, what were dachshunds originally bred for? Or a gerbil: where did gerbils come from?

This information will help you write your pet's character.

2 **Make a timeline.** Now make a timeline of the pet's life: when it was born, when it came to live with you, and the date now.

Add other events that your pet was around for (such as a birthday party, wedding, or someone being sick). What would these have been like from the pet's point of view?

3 **Use your imagination.** Now you can write your pet's life story, combining big events in its life with things it might have witnessed.

Use your imagination: the great thing about pets is, they never say you've got something wrong.

28. Make your own comic

ALL YOU NEED:
- Imagination
- Paper (lots)
- Pencils and pens
- Eraser

Making your own comic can easily take a whole day (or more). But if it looks like the sun might come out soon, you can also make it a quick activity.

1 **Find a subject.** What is your comic going to be about? Here are some other subjects (but feel free to choose your own):
- Discovering you have superpowers
- A bully getting their comeuppance
- Your pet
- A boring lesson that goes wrong in a funny way

2 **Develop a storyline.** Now turn your basic idea into a storyline, divided up into periods of time. Say you're making a cartoon of your pet's life story:
- **A** Max is one of six dachshund puppies
- **B** Max comes to live at his new home with us
- **C** He grows up
- **D** Max is now four years old

3 **Think of drawings.** What will you draw for each stage of your story?

You might have lots of things you want to draw about Max coming to live with you (he peed on the floor, he slept on your bed, he went for his first walk on the leash).

Make quick sketches of each scene and lay them out. Do they tell the story as you imagined?

4 **Plan your storyboard.** The next step is to decide how to lay out your cartoon. Some of the pictures might be funny or full of action and need lots of space—maybe even a full page.

Draw out the panels on each page, showing where each drawing goes and how big it will be.

5 **Add drawings.** Once you are happy with the layout, add the drawings (based on the sketches you did earlier) and words. Sometimes, it's a good idea to add the words first.

6 **Color in.** Adding color will make your comic really stand out.

7 **Draw a cover.** The last step is to name your comic and draw a cover for it. Once this is finished, staple or fold the whole comic together and it is finished.

ONLINE COMIC CREATION

There are comic-book websites that can be fun to use: try pixton.com or toondoo.com, for example. We think it's more fun to do the whole process yourself on paper, though!

1

2 CHOOSING
NEW PUPPY
TRAINING
SECRET POWERS
ADVENTURE!
RESCUE?

3

4 SUPER NOODLE
POW
THE END
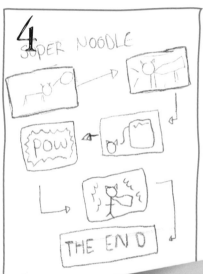

5

6

SUPER NOODLE!

Don't forget to leave space to add words!

29. Play "threes"

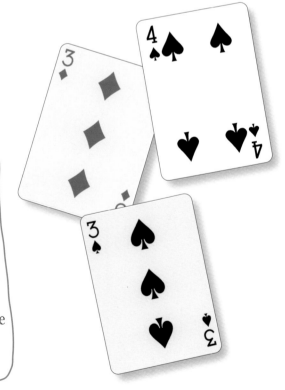

ALL YOU NEED
- Pack of cards
- At least two people

Threes is a card game. Once you learn the rules it is very difficult to stop playing. The basic idea is to get rid of all your cards as soon as you can.

1 Deal. Deal out three cards per player, face down. Then deal three on top of these, face up. Finally, deal each player three more cards, face down, which they can pick up.

  If they want to, players can now swap picked-up cards with face-up ones.

2 Play. The player with a black 3 goes first. If no one has one, it's the player with a red 3, a black 4, a red 4, etc.

  The first player lays down a card, then picks one up from the cards that didn't get dealt. The player to their left then has to lay a card with the same value or higher.

  Except...

3 Picking up. If a player cannot go, they have to pick up the whole pile of cards and add them to their hand.

4 Out. Once all the cards in the leftover pile are gone, you play the cards in your hand, then the ones lying face up, then the ones lying face down. No one can look at what the face-down cards are before playing them.

  When all your cards are gone, you are out. The last player still in loses.

SPECIAL CARDS
- 2s can always be put down
- 4s can always be put down and have the same value as the card beneath them
- on a 7, the next player has to lay the same (or lower)
- 10s can always be played: the whole pile is taken out and the player lays a new card

30. Go for an outdoor swim (You're wet anyway...)

ALL YOU NEED

- Swimsuit
- Towel
- Warm clothes

On a really rainy day, you can't really go for a hike, a bike ride, or a visit to the park. What you could do, though, is go for an outdoor swim.

1 **Pick a spot.** One of the best places for an outdoor swim is an open-air pool. You can get changed in the dry—your clothes will still be dry when you get out.

2 **Check the temperature.** Splash a bit of water onto your chest and face to make sure the water is not too cold.

3 **Feet first entry**. In a pool, follow the lifeguard's instructions for getting in. Elsewhere, always get in feet first. Every year people hurt themselves seriously by diving into unfamiliar water.

4 **Enjoy your swim!** Floating on your back with the rain falling on your face and rainwater trickling into your mouth is a great feeling.

WATER SAFETY

Never swim in the sea, a lake, or river unless you are 100 per cent sure it's safe. Make sure one of your parents knows where you are going and has said it's OK.

31. Do an experiment

ALL YOU NEED

- Large bowl
- 1 lb (450 g) cornstarch
- 2 cups (475 ml) water
- Spoon
- Clear, resealable plastic bag
- An egg (not cooked)
- Food dye

When is a liquid not a liquid? When it's something called a "non-Newtonian liquid," that's when. This experiment will show you how these liquids work.

1 Mix ingredients. Put the cornstarch into the bowl. Add the water and mix it in using your fingers. (Adding food dye to the water first makes colored slime.)

2 Get the mixture right. Keep mixing until the slimy liquid is like runny honey. If it's not quite thick enough, add more cornstarch to make the slime thicker. If it's too thick, adding more water will make it thinner.

Now you are ready to do some experiments.

3 Scoop it. Scoop some of the slime into your hand and roll it into a ball. As long as you keep pressure on it, it stays ball-shaped. Stop pressing, though, and it will flow back into the bowl.

4 Whack it. Try quickly punching the surface of the slime. Most fluids would splash, but not this one. Your punch's force pushes water away, leaving just a dense patch of cornstarch below your fist.

5 Do one last eggs-periment. Spoon some of the slime into the resealable bag until it is two-thirds full. Now gently push an uncooked egg into the mixture.

Make sure the bag is really tightly sealed, then find somewhere you can safely drop it from about 10 feet (3 m) up. Now drop the bag—what happens to the egg?

MESS ALERT
Making cornstarch slime can get messy. Of course, that might not bother you.

NON-NEWTONIAN LIQUID DISPOSAL

If you pour your slime down the sink when you're done, there is a good chance it will block the pipes and you'll be in massive trouble. To avoid this, spoon the mixture into a sealable bag (or two) and put it in the trash.

In a normal, Newtonian liquid such as water, the egg would break. In this non-Newtonian liquid, though, as the bag hits the ground the slime becomes solid around the egg. The force of the landing is evenly distributed around the shell's surface and it stays intact.

32. Make a kite

ALL YOU NEED

- Thick plastic bags (at least 3 x 1½ feet/ 1 x 0.5 m)
- Scissors
- Flying line from a kite shop
- Electrical tape
- 2 x wooden ¼-inch (5 mm) dowels, 3 feet (1 m) in length
- Marker pen

Sure, you could go to a store and buy a kite. But making a simple one is quite easy, and flying a kite you made yourself is great fun.

1 **Mark out your kite.** Measure 3 feet (1 m) along the side of one bag and put a dot at each end. Measure down 10 inches (25 cm), then 20 inches (50 cm) in, and mark that place with a dot, too. Draw lines between the top, middle and bottom dots.

10 in (25 cm) 30 in (75 cm) 20 in (50 cm)

2 **Cut out the shape.** Cut out along the two lines, then open out the shape: this is your kite.

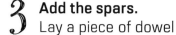

3 **Add the spars.** Lay a piece of dowel from the tip to the tail of the shape. Fold a 4-inch (10 cm) length of electrical tape over the dowel and on to the plastic to hold each end in place. Repeat for the cross spar.

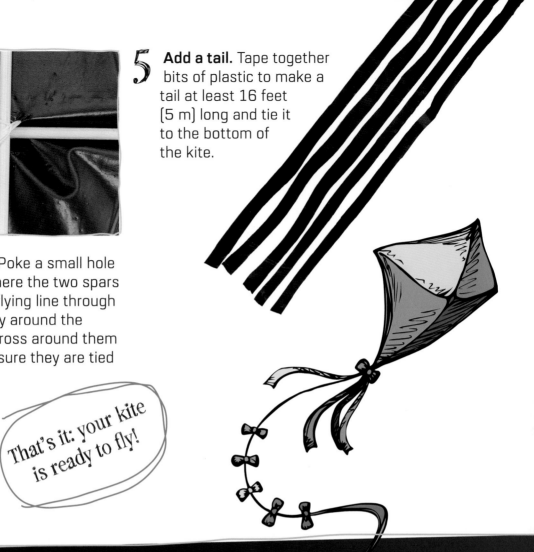

5 **Add a tail.** Tape together bits of plastic to make a tail at least 16 feet (5 m) long and tie it to the bottom of the kite.

4 **Tie on the line.** Poke a small hole in the plastic where the two spars cross. Push the flying line through and tie it securely around the spars (go criss-cross around them four times to be sure they are tied together).

That's it: your kite is ready to fly!

33. Say hello in five languages

Knowing a few words in a foreign language can come in handy. The first word most people learn in a new language is "hello."

Here's how to say hello in five of the world's six most commonly spoken languages. (We left out English, the third most common language: if you are reading this, you must already know that one.)

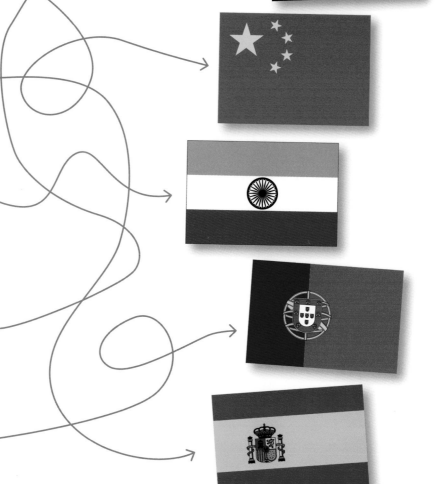

1 Mandarin Chinese.
Saying hello: *Nǐ hǎo*
Sounds like: **NEE how**

2 Spanish.
Saying hello: *Hola*
Sounds like: **OH-laa**

4 Hindi.
Saying hello: *Namaste*
Sounds like: **NAM-ahs-tay**

5 Arabic.
Saying hello: *marHaban*
Sounds like: **mer-HAB-ben**

6 Portuguese.
Saying hello: *Olá!*
Sounds like: **OH-la**

34. Learn some Makaton

Makaton is a simple, international form of communication. It is sometimes used by people with autism or Down syndrome, but anyone can learn it.

GOOD

OK

HELLO
Using both hands means "very good"

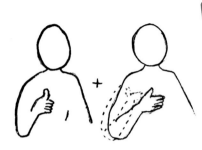

GOOD MORNING
A thumbs-up followed by touching your chest with your fingertips

GOODBYE
Wave your hand from side to side

PLEASE

THANK YOU
Please is halfway down; thank you is down to stomach level

YES
Tilted forward from the wrist

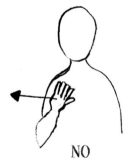

NO
Hand waved out to the side

COME
Pointer finger moves in the direction requested

GO
Pointer finger moves in the direction requested

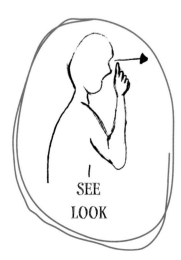

SEE

LOOK

DRINK

SLEEP

DINNER
Bring your right hand to your mouth twice, with the fingertips touching

35. Write a team poem

This is a fun activity with up to four friends. You are going to write a five-line poem called a limerick together.

Remember, limericks are sometimes called nonsense poems—so your poem doesn't have to make total sense. The first, second, and fifth lines have eight or nine syllables, and the third and fourth lines have five or six.

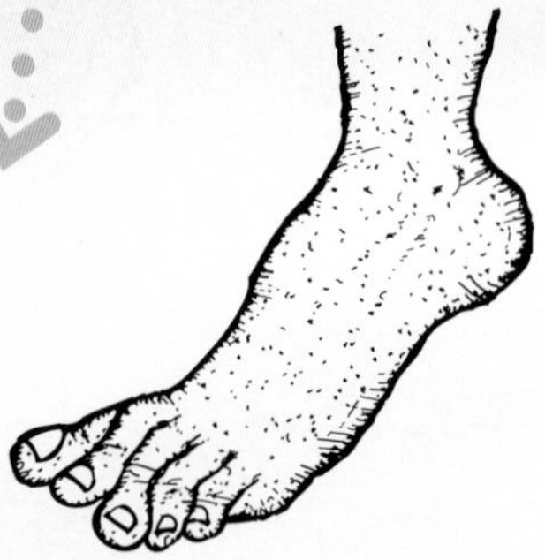

1 **Pick a subject.** One of you picks a subject and says or writes the first line to start things off:

I'd rather have fingers than toes

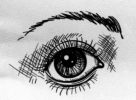

2 **Rhyme the last word.** The next person makes up the second line, ending with a word that rhymes.

I'd rather have eyes than a nose

3 **Introduce a new rhyme.** The third line must not rhyme with the two that went before:

And as for my teeth

4 **Add a line.** The fourth player's line rhymes with the one before (teeth):

It's my strong belief

5 **Back to the start.** The last line should rhyme with the first two (toes and nose):

I'll be terribly sad when they goes.

This is not good English—but it is a good limerick.

36. Go on a damp-day creature hunt

Sometimes you've just GOT to get outside. Why not take someone on a hunt to discover which creatures don't mind when it's wet?

ALL YOU NEED

- Raincoats
- Notepad and paper
- Camera

1 **Pick an area.** Decide where to explore. Somewhere close by might be best, just in case you get completely soaked.

Will you make your creature hunt in a forest, a grassy area, or a city street? There are animals in all of them.

2 **Take photos and notes.** First, just wait and look around. What animals can you see? There will probably be birds, flying insects, pets, and maybe more. Take photos and notes, for example:

Photo 1: brown freckled bird, pointy beak
Behavior: pecking at grass
Notes: puffed-up feathers

After a while you could start exploring more. Look under rocks, in bushes, and even on buildings.

3 **Research what you have found.** When you get home, use your notes and photos to find out more about the animals you saw. Why were the bird's feathers puffed up, for example?

STAY SAFE

If you are exploring outside, make sure an adult knows where you are going and what time you will be back.

37. Visit a museum

A rainy day is a really good excuse to visit places you might not normally go—such as a little local museum you have always wondered about.

1 **Choose a museum.** First, you need to pick a museum to visit. Local councils can often tell you about nearby museums—and if you are lucky, it will be a quirky one...

> ... in Ulm, Germany, there's a museum of bread
>
> ... in Maidstone, England, they have a Dog Collar Museum
>
> ... maybe strangest is the Museum of Barbed Wire in La Crosse, USA.

2 **Check the details.** Find out when the museum is open and whether you have to pay to go in. You also need to work out how to get there.

3 **Food and drink.** Depending on how far away the museum is, you could plan a packed lunch or find out if it has a café.

38. Create a home movie theater

ALL YOU NEED

- TV and DVD/Blu-ray player
- Snacks
- Drinks
- Lots of cushions, pillows, and blankets
- Camping/yoga mats (optional)

Going to the movies with your friends is expensive. Maybe instead you could stay home and create your own movie theater?

1 **Pick a movie.** Actually, pick two, then ask your guests which one they would prefer. (With a choice of more than two they might never agree...)

2 **Arrange snacks and drinks.** Ask an adult what you can offer everyone to eat and drink. Maybe you could have:
- Sandwiches
- Popcorn
- Juice
- Pieces of fruit

3 **Set up the room.** This is a movie theater with a difference: you will all be lying down.

Everyone needs at least two cushions or pillows and a blanket. Camping or yoga mats will make the floor softer.

4 **Start the movie.** Once everyone is settled, click "play," lie back, and enjoy the movie.

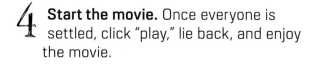

39. Become a yogi

A yogi is a person who does yoga. Yoga is a kind of exercise using strength, flexibility, and breathing. It can easily be done indoors.

1 Lie down. Lying down is a yoga position called corpse pose. Lie on your back, with your arms at your sides. Let your back relax against the floor. Stretch each leg away from you, then relax it.

2 Breathe in, then out. Breathe in deeply, letting your ribs and belly rise up as your lungs fill with air. Then breathe out slowly. Wait a moment before breathing in again. Do at least 10 deep breaths like this.

3 Cat pose. Kneel down with your toes pointing out behind you, then put your hands on the floor in front. They should be straight underneath your shoulders and your knees straight under your hips. Look at the floor.
Breathe in deeply. As you breathe out, bend your backbone toward the ceiling. When you breathe in again, slowly return to your starting position.

4 Cow pose. This has the same starting position as cat pose. As you breathe in, try to lift your chest and bottom toward the ceiling. This will drop your belly toward the floor. When you breathe in again, slowly return to your starting position.

5 Downward dog pose. Start as in the cow and cat poses, but with your hands a bit farther forward. Breathe out and lift your knees off the floor. Lift your bottom towards the ceiling. You are aiming to make a straight line from your hands to your bottom, and another from your bottom to your heels.

WATCH OUT

Never do a yoga pose so that it hurts, or feels like it is stretching you too much. If you ever feel uncomfortable, stop and gently return to a better position.

40. Bake some cakes

Maybe before your home movie theater event (page 47) you could bake some cakes for your guests? Everyone loves puffed rice cakes:

1 **Melt.** Put the chocolate, butter, and maple syrup into a heat-proof bowl and melt it. You can do this in 10-second bursts in a microwave, or by putting the bowl over a pan of boiling water.

2 **Stir.** Stir in the puffed rice. Some people add a few raisins or slices of dried apricot at this point, too.

3 **Make cakes.** Now divide your mixture into nine roughly equal parts and put them in cupcake cases. Put the cakes in the refrigerator for an hour, until they are cool and ready to eat.

INGREDIENTS:

- 3½ oz (100 g) broken-up milk chocolate
- 1¾ oz (50 g) broken-up dark chocolate
- 3½ oz (100 g) butter
- 4 tablespoons of maple syrup
- 3½ oz (100 g) puffed rice
- Paper cupcake cases

HELP NEEDED

This recipe involves hot liquids: always ask an adult to help, or at least watch what you are doing, when making this recipe.

41. Write a play

ALL YOU NEED

- Pen and paper, or a computer, to write things down

If a group of you is trapped by the rain, how about spending an afternoon writing a play?

1 Pick a subject. What is your play about? It could be a real event or a made-up one, but make it an interesting challenge (a mysterious theft, perhaps).

2 Decide the characters and setting. Make a list of the characters and what they are like. It could be historical, science-fiction, a robbery, or... Knowing what they are like will help you write their lines later.

Where is the play set? Is it where the theft took place, at the police station, or even in the getaway car?

3 Make a plot. Try this plan for your plot, separating the play into four parts:
- **A:** introduces the characters and the challenge they face
- **B:** events get more exciting... leading to a crucial dramatic moment
- **C:** the things that happen after the crucial moment, as things begin to slow down again
- **D:** how things end

4 Write the lines. Finally, use your plot to write what each character says and when they say it.

POLICE DEPT.
DATE:
06-07-2017
NUMBER:
XXX-XXXX-XXX

42. Produce a play

TOP TIP: In warm, dry weather, somewhere outside with blankets and cushions can be a great place to put on a play.

ALL YOU NEED

- A play
- Costumes
- Props
- Space
- An audience

Having written a play (page 54), you probably want to perform it. Getting ready to do this is called "producing" it.

1 **Hold auditions.** Auditions are where each person speaks the same lines by a character. Other people watch, then decide who is best for that role.

DIRECTOR

2 **Costumes and props.** Next you need to arrange costumes and props. Choosing your costume can be a great excuse to rummage around in the dressing-up box.

"Props" are the items actors need to play a part. Make a list of all the props you need. They could be things like a detective's badge, a gun, or a bottle of (not-really) drugged water.

3 **Set up the stage.** Decide where the play is going to be performed. Questions to ask:
- is there enough space?
- where will the actors come on stage from?
- is there room for the audience to sit comfortably?

4 **Check lighting.** After all your work, it is important that the audience can see the actors. Make sure they are well lit.

5 **Rehearse.** Rehearsing your play will help the actors remember their lines. It also shows if there is anything you have forgotten.

6 **Perform!** It might take quite a few rainy days before you are ready... but finally it will be time to gather your audience and perform the play.

43. Play rain races

The force of gravity means water flows downhill. It does not always flow at the same speed, though. This makes it possible to hold rain races with your friends.

Here are some possible rain races:

1 **Window races.** This is the simplest rain race and is a very quick activity. You and your friends each pick a raindrop that is near the top of the window. As soon as you pick, the race starts: whose raindrop gets to the bottom first?

2 **Poohsticks.** In the original version of Poohsticks, two sticks are dropped into a stream from one side of a footbridge. Then you cross to the other side and see whose stick comes out first.

If you do not have a footbridge nearby, or want the race to be a bit longer, just throw your sticks in the stream at a starting point, then run to a finishing line farther downstream and see who wins.

You don't need to go to the countryside to play Poohsticks

SAFETY CHECK

If you are playing near moving water (a stream or river), make sure an adult knows where you are going to be and has given you permission.

44. Go cloud spotting

If there is one thing you can be guaranteed on a rainy day, it is that there will be lots of clouds around. It's a good time to do some cloud spotting:

High clouds

Cirrus. High-up, wispy clouds that look stretched-out and thin.

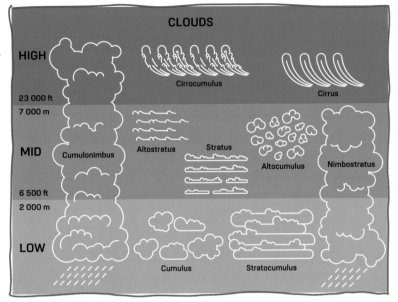

CLOUDS

HIGH

23 000 ft
7 000 m

MID

6 500 ft
2 000 m

LOW

Cirrocumulus

Cirrus

Cumulonimbus

Altostratus

Stratus

Altocumulus

Nimbostratus

Cumulus

Stratocumulus

Middle clouds

Altostratus. Thin clouds through which the sun can just about be seen.

Altocumulus. These clouds are thin like altostratus, but more broken-up in shape.

Low clouds

Cumulus. Cumulus clouds are heaped-up or puffy looking (a bit like cauliflower).

Nimbostratus. Flat-bottomed and heavy, these clouds deliver steady rain.

Cumulonimbus. Flat-bottomed clouds (often in the shape of an anvil) that stretch high up into the atmosphere. They can deliver lightning and heavy rain showers.

45. Measure rainfall!

On weather reports you might have heard people say things like, "There was ½ inch (10 mm) of rain last night." How do they know? They use a rain gauge—and now you can, too.

1 Prepare the bottle. To let water in, the top 8 inches (20 cm) of the bottle needs to be cut off in as straight a line as possible.

2 Cut the funnel to size. Adding a funnel stops water evaporating and means you will get a more accurate result.

First, put the funnel into the top of the bottle. If it doesn't fit, use the marker pen to draw a line on the funnel, where the top edge of the bottle touches it. Remove the funnel and cut along this line, then put the funnel back. It should now fit in the top of the bottle with no overlap.

3 Add pebbles and water. Now add about 4 inches (10 cm) of pebbles to the bottom of the bottle. These are to stop your rain gauge blowing over in wind. Next, pour just enough water into the bottle to completely cover the pebbles.

4 Mark off the gauge. Use a ruler to mark off ¼ inch (0.5 cm) intervals, starting with 0 at the level of the water and going almost to the top of the bottle.

5 Put your rain gauge outside. Find a spot where there is nothing except sky above the gauge. If you can find a place that's also out of the wind and direct sunlight, that is even better.

6 Record your data. If you want to know how much rain has fallen each hour, check the level every hour. (You could record daily or weekly rainfall instead, but it should always be an equal amount of time between checks.) Write down when the result was recorded and how much rain fell, like this:

Monday June 3, 18.00: ⅓ in (0.75 cm)
Tuesday June 4, 18.00: ⅔ in (1.5 cm)
and so on.

Once you have recorded each result, tip the water (but not the pebbles) out of the gauge, then top it back up to the zero mark.

7 Make a rainfall graph. Once you have all the results you want, make a graph. Along the bottom, put the times (the hour, day, or week). Up the side, put the amount of rain that fell into your gauge. Mark your results on the graph. You can present them as a line graph or a bar chart.

WATCH OUT

The cutting parts of this activity need quite a lot of force, so ask an adult to help you.

1

2

3

Also make
sure you have
permission to cut
up the funnel.

4

5

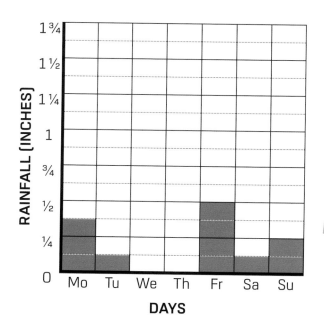

46–50. Five more things...

Here are five more things to try on a rainy day. For one or two of them you will need help (usually, help getting there or paying).

46 Set up indoor circuit training
You need someone with a big home for this! You could burn off some energy with sit-ups in the kitchen, push-ups in the lounge, jumping jacks in a bedroom, and running up and down stairs between each set of exercises.

47 Learn mirror writing
Mirror writing means the words only make sense when you look at them in reverse. Use a small mirror to practice writing your name in reverse, then start learning other letters.

48 Send coded messages
First, you need to make up a code, of course. A simple one is to write out the alphabet, then write numbers 1–26 above the letters. Now you have a simple number code.

1	2	3	4	5	6	7	8	9
A	B	C	D	E	F	G	H	I

10	11	12	13	14	15	16	17	18
J	K	L	M	N	O	P	Q	R

19	20	21	22	23	24	25	26
S	T	U	V	W	X	Y	Z

8-5-12-12-15

49 Decorate yourself
Not your actual self—an outline of it. Lie on a roll of art paper or some leftover wallpaper, then get someone to draw around you. Use glue to stick down old bits of cloth or candy wrappers to fill in the outline.

50 Go ice skating
If there is an indoor ice rink near you, it will probably be quieter than normal on a rainy day. After all, most people stay in when it's raining!

I wish it were sunny outside!

51. Play Desert Island Discs

This activity is inspired by a radio show that has been running in the UK since 1942. It is based on the idea that the guest has been marooned on a desert island.

1 **Pick eight tracks.** If you are playing this with a friend, decide who is the presenter and who is the guest.

   The guest (or "castaway") chooses eight songs that are important to her or him. Make up a playlist of the songs before you begin.

2 **Play the songs.** The presenter plays a bit of each song (not always the whole of it), then asks the guest why it is important. It might be because it is linked to happy or sad events, or because it reminds them of a person or place.

3 **Choose a book and a luxury.** As well as their eight tracks, the castaway is allowed to choose a book and a luxury to take to the desert island.

52. Tell a ghost story

ALL YOU NEED

- Imagination
- Pen/pencil and paper to write on (or a computer)

If you're camping (see page 81) or having a sleepover (page 84), nothing beats a good ghost story before bed. You could tell someone else's ghost story, taken from a library book. Or, you could make up your own:

1 **Pick a location and characters.** Maybe the story could be set among a group of campers or at a sleepover, for example?

2 **Decide what sort of story it will be.** Is the story going to be funny, scary or surprising? This will help you decide whether the ghost is friendly, a prankster, or just plain mean.

3 **Come up with a plot.** Your story needs:
- a *beginning*, which tells people where the story is happening and to whom
- a *middle*, which tells them what happens
- an *end*, which reveals how things turned out eventually

A good rule for stories is that each thing that happens should be a bit more interesting than what happened before.

53. Hold a tea party

ALL YOU NEED:

- Everyone's contact details
- Tea and soft drinks
- Sandwiches and cakes

Some kids only see relatives such as cousins at celebrations like Thanksgiving or weddings. If that's you, why not organize a cousins' tea party?

Tea Party
Sunday October 18
3pm
My house

RSVP

1 Pick a date. Pick a date for your party that gives everyone plenty of warning. About six weeks is usually enough. Send out invitations with the date, time, and place of the tea party.

2 Make a guest list. Once people have replied, you can write out a guest list. Use this to make sure you have enough chairs, plates, cups, etc.

TOP TIP

R.S.V.P. is short for *respondez s'il vous plait*—French for "please reply." Putting R.S.V.P. on invitations asks people to tell you whether they can come or not.

3 Decide your menu. A traditional tea-party menu would have tea, sandwiches and cakes. Add some alternative drinks for people who do not like tea.

4 Enjoy the party. Make sure the food is ready before everyone arrives, so that when they get there you can enjoy talking to them.

54. Play charades

Charades is a great game to play with your friends and relatives. The aim is to tell your teammates the name of a book, movie, play, or TV show without speaking.

1 **Pre-game planning.** You need two teams of roughly equal numbers. For each player on the opposing team, your team writes the name of a book, play, movie, or TV show on a piece of paper.

ALL YOU NEED:
- Pencil or pen
- Small pieces of paper

2 **Set up the act.** The first player is given a piece of paper by the opposition. She or he holds up fingers to show:

1] how many words there are to guess:

2] which word the player is starting with:

3] how many syllables are in the word:

= three words

= first word

= two syllables

CHARADES SIGNALS

Pulling your ear means "sounds like"

Holding fingers close together without touching shows it is a short word, such as "a"

Pointing at your chest means "I" or "me"

Pointing at someone while touching your nose means they have got a word right

3 **Start acting.** Now start acting the words. How would you act *The Cat in the Hat*, for example? Would you start with "cat," "hat," or one of the other words?

55. Hold a mini-Olympics

Holding a mini-Olympics is great fun with your friends OR your family. Just be careful about asking Grandma to do the long jump—unless she is a very active grandma, of course.

1 **Pick your events.** First you need to design your Olympic program of events. If everyone chooses one event (or two, or three, etc.), you should end up with at least one thing each Olympian enjoys.

SOME POSSIBLE EVENTS:

Running
You could have a sprint race from one place (the edge of a path, perhaps) to another (maybe a tree 110 yards/100 meters away). A longer race could be five times around the yard.

Timed shuttle runs
Set a starting line. Place one bottle 10 yards away, the next 20 yards away and the last 30 yards away. On "Go!" the stopwatch starts and the athlete runs to the first cone and touches it, runs back to the start, runs to the second cone and touches it, etc.

Once all the cones have been touched and the athlete gets back to the start line, the stopwatch is stopped. The fastest wins.

Long jumps
For the long jump you need two cones or plastic bottles about a yard apart. Spray a straight line of shaving foam between the two cones—if anyone's foot disturbs the shaving foam, their jump doesn't count.

Plank test

For this, you take turns holding the plank position, face-down with your toes and elbows on the ground and your legs and back in a straight line, for as long as possible. The one who lasts longest wins.

2 Check the ground.
Before you start, walk slowly around the "Olympic stadium." Look at the ground to check for deep holes that could trip someone, sharp stones or—worst of all—dog poop.

3 Agree the order and start competing.
Write down the order of competition. For events where you go one at a time, decide who goes first, second, etc. Keep to that order so that everyone gets the same amount of rest.

4 Make up a results table.
Write down the finishing order in each event. Give each person points: 1 for first, 2 for second, etc. At the end, add up the points: the person with fewest is the overall winner.

Now you are ready for the first event. Good luck!

RESULTS	1st	2nd	3rd
Run			
Long jump			
Shuttle run			
Plank test			

Overall:
1st _____
2nd _____
3rd _____

STAY SAFE!
Get permission from an adult to hold your mini-Olympics and make sure they know what all the events are going to be.

56. Rearrange your bedroom

ALL YOU NEED

- Pencil and paper
- Tape measure
- Ruler

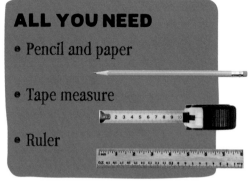

Rearranging your bedroom with your friends is a great way to get new ideas. They might come up with things you would not think of yourself.

1 Measure and draw a plan of your room.
First, measure your room from wall to wall.
Draw an outline of the room like this:
- For a room 98 inches (2.5 m) by 115 inches (2.9 m), you could decide that 10 inches = 1 inch. Use the ruler to draw a 9.8 x 11.5 inch (25 x 29 cm) rectangle.
  - Now measure and add the positions of doors and windows, plug sockets, etc.

2 Cut out your furniture. Not your real furniture—just shapes to represent it! For example, measure your bed. If it is 70 x 50 inches (1.8 x 1.3 m), draw a 7 x 5 inch (18 x 13 cm) rectangle on a new sheet. Write BED on it and cut out the shape. Do the same for things like closets, bureaus, tables, etc.

3 Rearrange. Now you can move the furniture in your room just by moving pieces of paper. Only move the ACTUAL furniture once you are happy with your new layout.

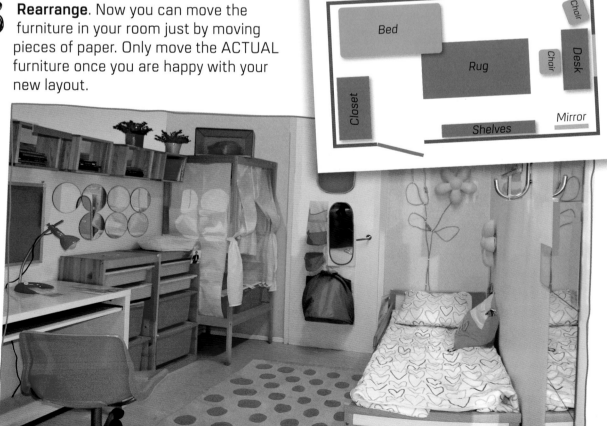

57. Make oat bars

If your friends have been helping you redesign your bedroom, maybe you could make them some oat bars to say thanks.

ALL YOU NEED

- 3½ oz (100 g) butter
- 3½ oz (100 g) light brown soft sugar
- 1¾ oz (50 g) maple syrup
- 7 oz (200 g) rolled oats
- Dried fruit, if you like it
- Baking pan
- Parchment paper

1 **Melt and mix.** In a large saucepan, melt the butter, sugar, and syrup. Once it has all melted, stir in the oats—and maybe dried fruit.

2 **Pour out.** Line a baking pan with parchment paper. Pour your mixture into the pan and press it down firmly.

3 **Cook and cut.** Put the pan in the oven for 10 minutes at 350°F (180°C). Take it out and allow it to cool for 10 minutes. Lift it out in the parchment paper, put it on a board, and cut into slices.

STAY SAFE!

You definitely need a adult with you when making oat bars. Some of the ingredients and equipment get really hot, which could be dangerous.

58. Interview your grandparents

ALL YOU NEED

- Pencil/pen and lots of paper

You might not know your grandparents as well as you think. These interview questions are guaranteed to reveal at least one thing you didn't already know.

1 **Where did you live until you were my age?** Even if they lived in the same town as you, you might not know exactly where. If they moved around, try pinpointing the places on a map. You might even be able to visit some of them.

2 **What was school like?** In your mind, compare their answer with what your school is like. (Tip: don't start telling them about your school. You are interviewing them, so your main job is to listen.)

3 **Tell me something surprising about when you were a kid.** Always save your trickiest question until last. This is when you have the best chance of getting a good answer. Your interviewee will have relaxed and got used to speaking about himself or herself.

TOP TIP

If your own grandparents are not available, borrow someone else's. Interviewing borrowed grandparents can be just as interesting, and even more surprising.

Draw a family tree

A family tree is a chart showing who is related to whom. You will probably need to speak to your parents, aunts, uncles, and grandparents to get all the information you need.

1 Start with you.
Draw yourself (and your sisters and brothers, if you have any) at the bottom of the paper. Add a note saying where you live.

2 Add your parents and grandparents.
Draw a line straight up from your name, leading to your parents' names. Put an equals sign between them: this is the family-tree symbol to show that people are together.

Do the same again with a line leading up from your parents to their parents (your grandparents).

3 Add aunts, uncles and cousins.
Now draw lines going down from your grandparents to their other children, if they have any. (These are your aunts/uncles.) Add their partners, then their children (your cousins).

You may be able to add even more detail than this, with great-grandparents, great-aunts/uncles, etc.

You might need a bigger piece of paper to fit them on, though!

59. Take a "Rembrandt" portrait photo

This is a kind of photo named after the famous Dutch artist Rembrandt. The faces of people in Rembrandt's portraits were often lit up like this.

ALL YOU NEED

- Camera
- Key light (shining through a window, from a lamp, or bright sunshine)

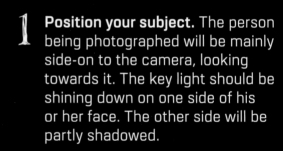

1. **Position your subject.** The person being photographed will be mainly side-on to the camera, looking towards it. The key light should be shining down on one side of his or her face. The other side will be partly shadowed.

2. **Fine tune.** Now have the person turn their head so that their nose casts a shadow. This shadow should link with the shadow on the side of their face. Just a little triangle of light will be left below their eye.

3. **Take the photo.** Take the photo and check it. Experiment with slightly different positions until you have a perfect Rembrandt-style portrait.

60. Take great selfies

Most people know how to take basic selfies. You hold the camera a little above you and look up before pressing the shutter button.

Here are three ways to take more interesting selfies:

1 **Use the timer**. Most cameras and phones have a self-timer button. Using this lets you put more of your surroundings (and fit more of your friends) into the photo.

2 **Use key light**. Key light that shines on the people, but leaves the background darker, can give your photos a big impact.

Light shining from above, with the person/people in the photo looking upwards, can also make a great photo.

3 **Choose your background.** Think about what is happening behind the person/people in the photo:

- If there is a lot to see in the background, it will distract from the portrait.
- If the background color is the same as the people (e.g. black hair and a black shirt with a dark background behind), the person/people might blend in and the portrait will not be as good.

61. Go fishing

If you have not tried fishing, maybe someone older in your family could take you? If you already know how to fish, though, you might be able to go with friends.

1 **Decide where to fish**. In most places, fishing in the sea is free. On rivers and lakes you sometimes have to pay.

A local fishing store might tell you good places to fish. They will also know what kind of fish there will be and what sort of bait you need.

2 **Preparation**. As well as your fishing gear, you need to pack a drink and, if you are going to be out for a while, something to eat.

Also take warm clothes if it's cold (fishing can involve a lot of standing/sitting around) or a hat/sunscreen if it's hot.

3 **Be patient**. If you don't catch a fish straight away, be patient. Spend half an hour at the spot you have picked before trying another one.

STAY SAFE

Alway make sure an adult knows you are going on a fishing expedition and has given permission. Tell them exactly where you will be and what time you will be back.

THROW BACK THE LITTLE ONES

Lots of anglers release all the fish they catch. If you do keep one to eat, make sure it is big enough—there are rules against keeping fish that are too small.

62. Save the planet before bedtime

Earth's population is constantly growing, but our planet is not getting any bigger. Each person needs to be more environmentally friendly. Here are four ways to do it:

1 **Take a shower.**
Showers use less water than baths*, so by showering you will be using less of Earth's precious water.
*Unless they are power showers, which can actually use MORE water than a bath. Turn the power-shower down to help save the world.

2 **Walk or cycle to school.**
Earth's temperature is slowly rising, causing destructive storms, melting ice at the Poles, and sea-level rises. This is partly caused by the gasses released by cars and other vehicles. Walking and cycling with your friends do not release these harmful gasses.

3 **Unplug cell phones once they are charged.**
To see why, unplug the charger from the outlet and hold it in your hand. The charger will be warm, which means heat energy is being wasted.
Producing energy releases the same harmful gasses as driving—so by saving energy, you will be helping to save the planet.

4 **Go veggie.** Crops such as vegetables and beans need less energy and water than meat. You don't need to go completely veggie, but eating less meat will help the planet.

63. Hold a Day of the Dead festival

The Day of the Dead is when Mexican families gather together to honor those who have died. It is on November 2 each year.

The Day of the Dead is the final day of a festival that begins on October 31. The festival is a celebration with special food, drink, costumes, and decorations.

Day of the Dead face paint

For the festival, people sometimes decorate their faces to look like skulls. As it's a happy festival, they add colors and flower shapes.

1 **White base.** Use the sponge to put white face paint all over your face, except in a big circle around your eyes.

2 **Black details.** Change colors and fill the eye circles with black face paint. Use the brush to give yourself a black nose and lips, and add a horizontal "stitch" line from each corner of your mouth.

3 **Add flowers.** Add black outlines of flower-petal shapes around your eye "holes." Finally, fill in the petals with bright colors.

ALL YOU NEED

- White face paint
- Black face paint
- Black face crayon
- Colored face crayon
- Face-painting sponge
- Face-painting brush

Make *champurrado*

The Day of the Dead happens when the weather is getting colder. Many people drink champurrado, a thick chocolate drink, to warm themselves.

1 **Warm the milk.** In a medium-size pan, mix the milk with the sugar, cinnamon, and chocolate. Warm it up and let it steam until the sugar and chocolate dissolve. This will take 5–10 minutes.

2 **Make the thickener.** Mix the cornstarch with the 2 cups of water until all the lumps have dissolved. Use a strainer if you need to get rid of any lumps.

3 **Mix carefully.** Add the cornstarch mixture to the pot and stir. Keep the heat low and keep stirring for another 8–10 minutes. Once the drink is nice and thick, it is ready to serve.

ALL YOU NEED

- 4 cups milk
- 2 cups water
- 1 thick stick of cinnamon
- three ½ oz (15 g) tablets of Mexican chocolate
- 6 oz (170 g) whole cane sugar
- ½ cup cornstarch

WATCH OUT!

Get an adult to help you make *champurrado*. Be careful while serving and drinking it: it will be hotter than you think.

64. Play "five dishes"

All you need for this activity is to like eating food. It is a good idea to play this just before mealtimes, as you are bound to end up feeling hungry!

1 **Rules**. The idea of this game is to pick your five favorite dishes. These are the ones you'd choose if you could only ever eat five different plates (or bowls) of food again, for the rest of your life.

2 **Pick your dishes**. Go round your group of friends, picking one dish each and writing down your choice. Write whether it is a first course, an entrée or a dessert.

   Keep going round until everyone has chosen five dishes.

3 **Make a menu**. Now you all get to agree on a menu. List all the first courses and vote for which people like best. Then pick an entrée and a dessert.

   Maybe someone will even prepare the meal you have created.

TOP TIP!

Even if desserts or burgers are your absolute favorite, don't pick five different kinds. You would get bored of them in the end.

65. Go on a shooting-star expedition

Shooting stars—also called meteors—are not actually stars at all. They are bits of space rock. As they enter Earth's atmosphere they burn brightly before being vaporized.

1 **Pick a time**. Shooting stars can only be seen at night. You are most likely to see them during a "meteor shower." An internet search for "next meteor shower" should tell you when would be a good time.

2 **Pick a place**. To see shooting stars you need to be somewhere that the sky is very dark. An ideal place is on a high hill in the countryside. (Always make sure you are allowed on the land.)

3 **Set up**. Lay your tarp on the ground, then the blankets, and lie back looking up at the sky. It's best to concentrate on one area for a few minutes: using binoculars might help you to do this.

66. Run a water-balloon relay

ALL YOU NEED
- Balloons
- Water

TOP TIP
This is definitely an outside game. If you live somewhere cold, only run the water-balloon relay in summertime!

This is a relay race with an added twist—because every player has to get wet to complete the relay. It is great fun on a really hot day.

1 **Prepare the balloons.** Fill the balloons with water. Don't put so much in that they are almost bursting: fill them so that there's a bit of space near the opening and you can tie the baloons easily. You need two balloons for each person.

2 **Set out the course**. Put half of each team's balloons in a row at the start line and half at the finish line. Make sure it's clear which balloons belong to which team.

3 **Race!** On GO! the first player runs out to the balloons, sits on one to pop it, runs back and sits on another. Only when the second balloon is popped can the next player set off.
The first team to pop all their balloons wins. The prize is wet pants.

You're going to get wet. Maybe not this wet, though.

67. Go camping for the weekend

Whether it is with your friends, family or both, a camping trip is a great way to spend time together. (If you want it to be really different, try making it a digital-free weekend.)

1 **Pick a place.** The easiest place to hold a camping weekend is at a proper campsite. But some families use a big yard, borrow a field, or camp in the wild instead. That way they have the space to themselves.

2 **Make preparations**. There's a well-known saying: "Proper preparation prevents poor performance." When you're going camping, this is definitely true.

Before the weekend, make a checklist of things to take. When you pack, tick them off to make sure you have everything.

3 **Setting up your tent.** Putting up your tent in the right place can make a big difference to how well you sleep. Here are a few things to check:
- Is the ground level? You can test this by lying down on it. Try lying in different directions to decide which way your tent should face.
- Are there any sticks or stones there? Move them, or they could damage the floor of your tent (or your back!).

4 **Enjoy the weekend.** This book should have given you lots of ideas for things to do while you are away. You could also look at *Things To Do Outdoors* for even more suggestions.

MY CAMPING WEEKEND: PERSONAL THINGS
√ Sleeping bag
√ Pillow (v. important!)
√ Air bed
√ Book to read
√ Flashlight to read it with
√ Beanie hat in case cold
√ Clothes for 3 days (2 days + 1 in reserve!)
√ Raincoat/umbrella

GET PERMISSION!
If your group is planning to set up the tents in a field or anywhere that isn't an official campsite, make sure you are allowed to camp there.

68. Play the five-word game

The five-word game is a storytelling game, where each person tells part of a story using only five words. The story can turn out to be funny, spooky, exciting—whatever the players decide. It could start like this:

Player 1 — "The huge wave crashed ashore..."

Player 2 — "... it raced up the beach..."

Player 3 — "...there goes the picnic lunch..."

Player 4 — "... thought Vampire Beatrice as she..."

Player 1 (again) — "... looked up from the tasty..."

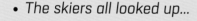

Here are a few more ideas to get you started:

- The skiers all looked up...
- Only one person noticed that...
- "Not again!" thought the Stegosaurus...
- Even in daylight, a leopard...

69. Plan a sleepover

ALL YOU NEED

- Food and drink
- Entertainment
- Sleeping bags and pillows (ask your guests to bring their own)

If it is your first sleepover, just invite two or three of your closest friends. Once you have more experience you will feel more confident about inviting more people.

1 **Pick some food**. The ideal food is simple and can be prepared before your guests arrive. Try to pick things you know most people like, instead of just your own favorites.

2 **Decide on entertainment**. You do not need to plan every minute, but it is a good idea to have thought of some games you can all play, a movie you are going to watch, or some other form of entertainment.

3 **Actually sleep.** It is called a sleepover, not an "awakeover"—you all need to go to sleep eventually.

If some people want to sleep sooner, let them. They are your guests, so you should make them feel comfortable.

TOP TIP

Some museums and zoos offer the chance for a sleepover inside. Imagine waking up among the dinosaurs, or next door to the lions!

70. Make a flatbread pizza

If you are having a sleepover, maybe you could make flatbread pizzas? Nearly all kids like pizza, so they would be a popular choice.

ALL YOU NEED

- Flatbread (Italian *piadina* is ideal)
- Olive oil
- Sun-dried and fresh tomatoes
- Olives
- Fresh basil
- Cheese (optional)

1 Prepare the ingredients. Cut up the fresh tomatoes. Slice the sun-dried ones into thin strips. Slice the olives. Chop up the fresh basil—not too small, though.

2 Assemble the pizzas. Lay out the flatbreads on a baking tray, then use a pastry brush to spread a small amount of olive oil on the tops.
Sprinkle the flatbreads thinly with tomatoes, olives and basil. Add a bit of grated cheese (if you like cheese).

3 Cook and eat. Put the pizzas in a hot oven (about 400°F/ 200°C) for 5–7 minutes. Take them out, wait 1 minute for them to cool down, then eat.

WATCH OUT!

Check with an adult whether you are allowed to use a sharp knife to cut up the ingredients.

71–76. Six more things...

You might need help from your parents for some of these activities... usually, help paying for them!

71 Ride a roller coaster
If you go for a thrilling roller coaster ride with other people, you will probably all be able to remember it years later. Not every single bit—it's usually too scary. But you will probably all remember that when it finished you were a) relieved, and b) disappointed.

72 Go to an outdoor movie
Some warm places have permanent outdoor movie screens. But even if you live somewhere cooler, there will probably be an outdoor movie screen somewhere nearby during summer. Take a blanket, loads of snacks, and something to drink.

73 Go for a bike ride
Riding on the road can be a bit dangerous and some parents don't like their kids doing it. So find an off-road cycle track (for example, along an old railway line) and set off on a two-wheeled expedition.

74 Make a drawing or painting
It doesn't have to be a pretty country scene. You could draw anything: a building, a car—or just use colors to paint what something feels like to you.

75 Learn to surf
Standing up on your first wave is unbelievable fun. Watching your friends falling off as they learn is possibly even more fun.

76 Have a dance party
Put on your favorite songs and show off your best dance moves. You could even make it a competition. Even better, why not choreograph a dance routine with your family or a group of friends?

77. Wash a car

ALL YOU NEED:

- Big, soft sponge
- Microfiber cloth
- Two buckets
- Watering can or hose
- Soft brush
- Car-wash liquid

Almost everyone likes it when their car looks clean. Maybe one of your neighbors is not able to wash their car, though. Why not offer to do it for them?

1 **Preparation**. Mix a bucketful of warm water and car-wash liquid, plus another bucket of cold water. Using the watering can or hose, wet the car down: this will soften up dried-on bugs and dirt.

2 **Get washing!** Start at the top, with the roof (you may need help from an adult to reach), so that the dirty water runs down over areas you have not washed yet. Keep rinsing out your sponge in the cold, clean water.

3 **Work your way down**. Next, wash the windows and upper panels, then go round the hood and lower body panels. The front might need two or three goes to get all the bugs off. Last, use the brush to clean the wheels.

4 **Rinse and dry.** Use the hose or watering can to rinse the car (again starting at the top). Wipe it dry with the microfiber cloth.

TOP TIP
Don't wash a car in bright sunshine. It dries too quickly and comes out looking smeared.

78. Add an interior valet

The only trouble with a newly washed car is that you cannot see the shine while you are in it. Giving the inside a good clean, too, is called "valeting" the car.

1 **Vacuum.** Use the small attachments to vacuum clean the carpets and seats. You can switch to the little brush attachment to clean the dashboard. Be careful, though: the plastic "glass" is easily scratched.

2 **Nooks and crannies.** Look at the nooks and crannies, such as the gap between the driver's seat and the door. These are hard to clean, because the vacuum cleaner won't fit in. Use a toothbrush to brush out the dirt, then vacuum it up.

3 **Wash down.** Wash down hard surfaces using a damp sponge with a TINY bit of dish soap on it. This will lift off any grease. Use the microfiber cloth rinsed in clean water to wipe the surfaces clean afterward.

WATCH OUT!
Never clean glass or clear plastic with dish soap: it will get scratched.

79. Make some thank-you cards

ALL YOU NEED:

- Thick paper/thin card
- Normal paper the same size
- Colored pens, tape, and other decoration
- An envelope

In every neighborhood there are people who do things for the community. Giving them a thank-you card you have made is sure to brighten up their day.

1 **Decide on a size.** How big will your card be? Tiny little cards are nice to get, and so are massive ones.

2 **Practice your design.** Before making the actual card, practice on a piece of normal paper. You can do this by folding it in half, then in half again.

   Your card could be:
   - Rainbow stripes
   - Polka dot patterns
   - A cut-out shape
   - Stuck-down scraps

   Or some other design you have come up with.

3 **Make the card.** Once you are happy with the design, recreate it on the actual card. Don't forget to put a message inside, such as, "Thanks for delivering our mail!"

Now put it in the envelope and hand it to the person you want to thank.

90

80. Offer library visits

This is a really easy way to help out a neighbor who finds it tricky to get around, perhaps because they are elderly or have a health problem.

1 **Visit**. Go and knock on their door (take your mom or dad with you first time) and explain that you are going to visit the local library: would they like you to bring them back any books?

2 **Make a list**. Write down the books your neighbor would like. It might be the exact books, or a kind of book (spy stories or romances, for example). You might also need to borrow their library card.

3 **Borrow the books**. Go to the library and borrow the books. If you are just looking for a particular type of book, explain things to the librarian. He or she will give you advice about what to borrow.

4 **Return or renew**. This is an important bit: do not forget, the books have to be returned or renewed! Make a note on the calendar of the day before they are due back, so you have time to collect them.

81. Oil a chain

Bicycles with rusty chains are harder to pedal and make a horrid squeaky-creaky noise. If you spot a local bike with a rusty chain, maybe you could oil it?

1 **Check the pedals**. You can usually oil a chain without moving the bike. Just carefully move the pedals backward with your hand to make sure you can spin them right around without catching them on anything.
   Turning the bike upside down makes this easier.

2 **Drop on the oil**. Slowly turn the pedals backward, adding one drop of oil to each link in the chain. When you get to an oily link, you will know you are back where you started.

3 **Wipe off any extra.**
   Now put a few drops of oil on your clean cloth. Hold the chain between your thumb and a finger, then slowly move the pedals backward. This spreads the oil out and removes any extra.

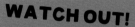

WATCH OUT!
Be very careful not to get your fingers caught while you are oiling or wiping the chain.

82. Adjust someone's bike gears

Sometimes when you are oiling a bike chain (see opposite), the gears keep clanking and getting stuck as you move the pedals. This is a sign there is something else you could do for the owner: adjust their gears.

1 Turn the bike upside down.
Put the bike upside down, balancing it on its handlebars and saddle. Turn the pedals forward and shift the bike into its lowest gear (the smallest cog at the back).

2 Screw in the adjuster. Where the gear cable goes into the derailleur (see below), there is a little adjuster that can be screwed in or out. Screw this as far into the derailleur as it will go.

3 Adjust the gear shift.
Now click the gear shifter one click, to try and make it go into second gear. Turn the pedals: the gear won't shift.

4 Get it changing smoothly. While turning the pedals, start unscrewing the adjuster. The chain will first start to jump, as if it is trying to shift up one gear. Then it will jump across. Unscrew the adjuster a little more, until the chain runs smoothly in second. Job done!

WATCH OUT!
Sometimes bikes stop changing gear properly because parts are worn out or damaged. If the tips on this page don't help, the bike might need to go to a bike shop to find out what's wrong.

83. Organize a soccer game

A soccer match is a great way for neighbors to get to know each other. On a nice day, why not try organizing a neighborhood soccer match?

1   **Decide who can play.** Your game might be for kids only. Everyone just turns up and you pick teams there.

   You could also invite special teams. For example, you could say that teams have to have a certain number of boys and girls, or that the team's total age has to add up to at least 50. For more complicated arrangements like this, people will need more warning.

DOUBLE CHECK
Make sure soccer is allowed at the place you have chosen for the match, as well as that no one else will be using it.

2 **Invite players**. Once you have decided who can play, and when and where the game will be, make some invitations and notices:

You could put invitations through people's doors, pin notices on posts, or do both.

NEIGHBORHOOD SOCCER!

All neighborhood kids invited

When:
this Sunday, June 29

Where:
Barn Walk Playground

3 **Make it a tournament**. If you have enough players, you could make it a tournament with three, four, or five players per team.

84. Tidy a yard

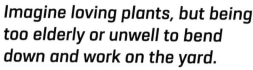

ALL YOU NEED:

- Gardening or safety gloves
- Rubber boots (if it's wet or soggy)
- Gardening tools
- Trash bags

Imagine loving plants, but being too elderly or unwell to bend down and work on the yard.
If that describes any of your neighbors, tidying up their yard would be a very good deed indeed.

1 Get permission. First, of course, you need to make sure your neighbor WANTS their yard tidied.
Yard tidying is much easier in a crew, so it would be a good idea to get some of your friends to come and help, too.

2 List your jobs. Make a list with your neighbor of what they would like done. Gardening is hard work, so separate the jobs into one-hour blocks of time:

Hour 1: Clear out dead leaves and fallen branches from flower bed
Hour 2: Water plants with mixture of water and plant food
Hour 3: Use leaf-blower to clear the front driveway; rake leaves into pile ready for bonfire.

TOP TIP

As well as being hard work, gardening can be dirty work—so don't wear your finest fashion gear!

WATCH OUT!

If you are tidying someone's yard, double-check before cutting down any plants. Chopping down a neighbor's favorite flower bush would NOT be a good deed!

(Always put a fun job at the end: it helps you get through the other ones.)

85. Take out the trash/recycling

This is a good deed you can do for neighbors who find it hard to get around. Elderly people, for example, might find it difficult to carry heavy trash bags.

1 **Get together a client list.** Talk to your parents about whether any of your neighbors might appreciate help with their trash or recycling. Go round to see them and ask.

2 **Take out the trash/recycling.** On the correct day (if there is a collection day where you live), go round and put out the trash/recycling. You could offer to check the recycling to make sure everything is allowed, too.
If you are moving trash bags, take some spare ones in case any split!

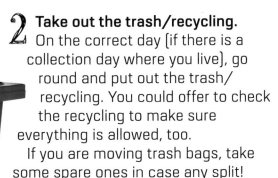

3 **Bonus good deed.** Trash is sometimes collected from trash cans people leave out on the curb. If you see these have been left out, you could drag them back on to your neighbor's property for them.

Of course, taking out the trash is not the only chore you could do for a neighbor. If it snows in winter, how about clearing the path to their front door, for example?

86. Compare childhoods

ALL YOU NEED:
- List of questions or topics
- Something to record answers (optional)

This is a good activity to do with neighbors who were born a long time before you. If you speak to someone who was a child in a different country, their story may be even more interesting.

1 **Questions or topics**. Before you speak to your neighbor, think about some of the things that most kids experience. They might include:
School
Toys, games, and sports
Food
Your bedroom/where you sleep
Festivals and holidays

When you speak, these topics might be helpful—you could even turn them into a list of questions.

2 **Write a report**. If you have a school magazine or a neighborhood newsletter, you could write a report about what it was like being a kid in your neighbor's time.

TOP TIP

If you are writing an article, make sure you show it to your neighbor before sending it to anyone else. This gives them a chance to say if they are happy with it and to correct any errors.

87. Clean some windows

Everyone likes having clean windows, but not many people enjoy cleaning them. Window cleaning is a quick, easy job you can do for your neighbors.

ALL YOU NEED:

- An old sponge
- Bucket of warm water and a squirt of dish soap
- Squeegee
- Bucket of clean, cold water
- Two microfiber cloths

1 **Buffing**. Buff the warm, soapy water on to the window with the sponge, making sure every bit gets wet. Do one window at a time, otherwise some will dry out before you get to them.

TOP TIP!
Good squeegee technique is the key to good window cleaning! It needs to be angled slightly as you wipe across, so that the wiped-off water trickles down the window.

2 **Squeegee**. Starting at the top of the window, wipe across with the squeegee. Overlap your wipes slightly so that each lower wipe covers the bottom bit of the one above.

3 **Wet cloth**. Now use a wrung-out, damp microfiber cloth to wipe the whole window clear of smears and marks.

4 **Dry cloth**. Use your dry cloth to give the window a final polish.

88. Bake a cake

If you know it's a neighbor's birthday, how about baking them a special surprise? They'll really appreciate it.

ALL YOU NEED:

For the cake:
- 7-inch (18 cm) baking pan
- Parchment paper
- 7 oz (200 g) carrots
- 6 oz (175 g) soft brown sugar
- 7 oz (200 g) self-rising flour
- 1 tsp baking soda
- 2 tsp cinnamon
- zest of an orange
- 2 eggs
- 5 fl oz (150 ml) sunflower oil

For the icing:
- 1¾ oz (50 g) softened butter
- 2¾ oz (75 g) confectioners' sugar
- 7 oz (200 g) cream cheese

1 **Preparations**. Line a 7-inch (18 cm) square pan with parchment paper. Turn the oven on to 350°F (180°C).

2 **Get grating**. Grate the carrots using the fine side of the grater (the one with the small holes). Next, tip the grated carrot into a big bowl.

3 **Add ingredients**. Using a strainer to make sure there are no lumps, put the sugar, flour, baking soda, and cinnamon on top of the carrot. Next, add the orange zest and mix it all together.

WATCH OUT!
When you are using a grater and an oven, make sure an adult has given you permission or is there to help.

4 **Add eggs**. Break the eggs into a bowl (watch out that no bits of shell get left in), then add them and the oil to the other ingredients. Mix everything together well.

5 **Bake!** Pour the mixture into the pan and make sure it is level at the top. Put it in the oven for 30 minutes or until it is brown on top, then take it out and let it cool down.

6 **Make icing**. While the cake is cooking, you can make icing. Mix the butter and confectioners' sugar together, then stir in the cream cheese until it is all smooth.

7 **Ice, cut, share out.** When the cake is cool, spread icing on top. Cut the cake into squares, ready to share out. You could deliver them to your neighbors in little paper bags.

89. Provide pet help

ALL YOU NEED:

* Neighbors with pets

If you are someone who likes animals, this is something you can do to help your neighbors that is also a lot of fun.

DOUBLE CHECK

Before offering to look after someone's pet, speak to your parents and make sure they would be happy for you to take on the job.

1 **Offer to help**. You could offer to help in lots of different ways, from walking someone's dog to feeding a cat, or looking after a pet hamster while its owner is on vacation.

2 **Get to know the pet**. If you don't already know it, make sure the pet you are looking after likes you and you like it. Big pets like dogs need to be kept under control and good at walking on the leash.

3 **Make a list**. With the owner, make a list of the things you need to do to look after their pet:

Horatio the Hamster
- *clean water every morning*
- *give food between 6 and 7 every night*
- *clean out cage Monday, Wednesday, Friday*
- *DO NOT allow to escape, he hides!*

WATCH OUT!

If you are looking after someone else's dog, never let it off the leash— it might run away and not come back!

90. Organize a kids' walk

Walking together is a great way to get to know people. There is something about walking that often makes people talkative.

ALL YOU NEED:
- Comfortable shoes
- Small backpack
- Food and drink, or money
- Cell phone

1 **Plan your route**. It could start with collecting everyone. The route could start at one of your homes, then go to the next-nearest person's house to get them, the next nearest, and so on.

   Once you have collected everyone, where will you go? Start with a short walk, about 2½–3 miles (4–5 km) away. This means you will be walking 5–6 miles (8–10 km) in total.

2 **Make sure you have enough time**. You will need to make sure you get home in time. But if your walk is 5½ miles (9 km) long, there and back, how long will it actually take you?

   Most people walk at about 3 mph (5 kph) on flat ground. So a 5½ mile (9 km) walk will probably take a bit over 2 hours (allow a bit of time for stopping).

10.30–11.00 Collect walkers
11.00 Set off to soccer match
12.15 Arrive at soccer field
12.30–2.30 Watch game
2.45 Set off for home
4.00–4.30 Drop off walkers

WHERE TO WALK?
Your walk does not have to be in the countryside. You could just as easily walk through town—to a museum, art display, or sports contest, for example.

3 **Draw up a schedule**. Your schedule might look like this. If you leave this with a parent, they will know where you are supposed to be and what time to expect you back.

4 **Pack your backpack**. Take something to drink and some food, or money to buy these things if there will be stores. Take the right clothes, too: a wooly hat and sweater if it is cold, or sunscreen and a sun hat if it is hot, for example.

91. Have a street party

A street party for neighborhood kids is a great way to help everyone get to know each other. All you need is a time, some food and drink, and maybe some music.

1 **Get helpers!** Organizing a neighborhood party is a job for a team of people, not just you. Get your friends and parents involved.

2 **Set the time and place.** Decide when the party will be—Halloween or Midsummer's night, for example. Put up notices and tell as many other kids as you can find.

Hope for dry weather, because nothing spoils an outdoor party like rain!

3 **Divide jobs.** One person could be in charge of food, with other people doing music playlists, drinks, etc.

Street-party food: Pinwheel pizzas

ALL YOU NEED

For the pizza dough:
- Olive oil
- 1 lb 2 oz (500 g) pack bread mix flour
- 1¾ oz (50 g) cheddar, grated

For the filling:
- 4 tablespoons tomato paste
- Handful of basil
- 1 whole roasted pepper
- 2½ oz (70 g) sun-dried tomatoes, chopped up
- 4½ oz (125 g) ball mozzarella, torn into chunks
- 10-inch (25 cm) springform pan

Pinwheel pizzas are a great snack for a street party. They are really easy to make (though you might want an adult to help you with some bits).

WATCH OUT!
If your party is going to actually block the street, you will need to get permission. Ask your parents to help with this.

1 **Preparation**. Oil a 10-inch (25 cm) springform pan. Make up the bread mix into dough, following the instructions on the packet.

2 **Roll out the dough**. Put the dough on a lightly floured surface, then use a rolling pin to roll it out to roughly 14 x 8½ inches (35 x 22 cm).

3 **Add filling**. Spread tomato paste over the dough, but leave a clear strip around the edge. Scatter the basil, pepper, sun-dried tomato, and mozzarella over the top.

4 **Roll up.** Roll up the dough from the longest side. Now slice it into eight thick pinwheels. Put seven of them around the edge of the tin, with the eighth in the middle. Cover the tin with plastic wrap and leave it in a warm place until it expands and looks much bigger. (This can take up to an hour.)

5 **Cook, cool, eat.** Heat the oven to 475°F (240°C). Remove the plastic wrap, scatter cheddar cheese on top and cook for 12–15 minutes, until golden. Remove from the oven and let them cool down a bit before eating.

92. Grow some food (and give it away)

ALL YOU NEED

- Old yogurt pot
- Cotton balls
- Paper towels
- Cress seeds
- Water
- Colored pens

Not just any food: you are going to grow Mr (or Ms) Cresshead. This is bound to make your neighbors smile.

1 **Prepare your pot.** Take the label off and paint a funny face on the front (practice on a bit of scrap paper first). Put a wet paper towel at the bottom of the pot, then some damp cotton balls on top. The cotton balls need to come almost to the top.

2 **Plant your seeds.** Sprinkle some cress seeds on top of the cotton balls and press them down a bit (not too hard, though).

3 **Position your pot.** Put the pot somewhere sunny and warm, such as on a windowsill.

4 **Deliver Mr (or Ms) Cresshead.** After about a week, the cress seeds will have grown into green "hair" for Mr (or Ms) Cresshead.
   Now deliver it to one of your neighbors, to cut off and put on an egg salad sandwich.

93. Give stuff away

You probably have old toys, clothes, and sports equipment you do not use any more. Maybe some of it would be useful for younger local kids?

1 **Work out what you no longer need.** Some things are easy. You can no longer need a coat you have outgrown, for example—it just won't fit you.

With toys and sports equipment, it is harder to decide. Will you really never want a particular game or book again? A good guide is to think when you last used it. If it was over a year ago, you probably don't need it any more.

2 **Set up a stand.** On a dry day, set up a stand outside your home. You need a little table, or a box with the items inside.

Add a sign saying HELP YOURSELF.

If you want to meet the kids who get to use your stuff, you could sit outside and meet them.

DOUBLE CHECK

Before you give anything away, check with your parents first. They might be annoyed if you get rid of something they planned to give to your little brother/sister/cousin.

HELP YOURSELF

WATCH OUT!
Once you have given something away, you cannot get it back. Make sure you are SURE you won't want it any more.

94. Set up a trash hunt

ALL YOU NEED
- Volunteers
- Trash bags

One thing you can do for ALL your neighbors is tidy up your area. On windy days especially, bits of trash get blown around and scattered everywhere.

1 **Get a team of hunters together.** The more of you there are, the easier the trash hunt will be. Maybe you could get everyone from your walking group (see page 103)—you know they like being outdoors!

2 **Make tidy packs.** You could work in packs of two, one with a sack for recyclable waste and the other for trash. Or there could be three per pack, with one person each for paper, plastic, and trash.

3 **Remove the trash.** The actual trash needs to go in a trash can. If you have found anything containing chemicals, such as old batteries, these usually need to be put in a special waste bin.
    The recyclable waste should go into paper or plastic recycling bins.

4 **Say thank you.** If you want people to help you again, always make sure you thank them for helping this time. As a reward for everyone who helped with the tidy-up, maybe you could have some of the cake from page 100, or the pinwheel pizzas from page 104?

TRASH DISPOSAL
Check with the local council what you should do with the trash you find. Plastic, glass, and paper should be recyclable, and sometimes other things are.

95. Make an "I can do it" flyer

ALL YOU NEED
- Paper
- Pencil and colored pens
- Photocopier or printer

Pick the ideas in this book that you like most. Perhaps you like the idea of dog-walking and window cleaning, for example. Make up a flyer to tell people about the things you can do for them.

1 **Decide what you are called.**
Maybe you decide to call yourselves Neighbor Angels or Help From the Hood, for example:

2 **Add your services.**
List the things you can do:

HELP from the HOOD

Dogs walked
Windows cleaned
Mornings, evenings,
and weekends
No window too small
(but some are too high...)

We are Pat and Nicki, two local 11-year-olds. If you have jobs you cannot do yourself, we will try to help!

Contact our parents on:
patandnickihoodhelpers@localmail.com

3 **Add a short description.**
Say a bit about what you offer, who you are, and how to find you (*always make sure people get in contact through your parents*)

96. Smile

This might be the most important of all the things you can do for your neighbors. It's amazing how much happier life is if people smile at each other—especially if they smile for no particular reason.

YOU COULD . . .

… smile when you pass on the street

… smile at people driving by (and wave, if you know them)

… smile at people in their yards

In fact, give people a nice smile whenever you get the chance. You are almost certain to get one back!

97–102. Six more things...

There is no need to stop at doing just 20 things for your neighbors—so here are six more!

97 **Eat lunch with a new kid**
Being at a new school can be scary—if you spot a new kid eating alone, sit beside them at lunch to make them feel welcome.

98 **Be an umbrella escort**
On a rainy day at the local store, offer to hold an umbrella over people as they take their shopping back to their car.

99 **Remember birthdays**
Make a little note on the calendar. Everyone loves getting an unexpected birthday card!

October

SUNDAY	MONDAY	TUESDAY	WEDNESDAY	THURSDAY	FR
	1	2	3	4	5
7	8	9 *Jim's birthday!*	10	11	12
14	15	16	17	18	19
21	22	23	24	25	2
28	29	30	31		

100 Say something nice
It could just be that you like someone's new haircut, or that their coat really suits them, or looks lovely and warm.

101 Be a good listener
The best way to get to know someone is to listen to them. Everyone in your local community will have their own stories, experiences, and knowledge to share. Listen carefully and ask them questions. There is no limit to what you might learn!

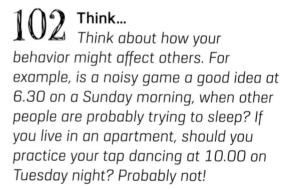

102 Think...
Think about how your behavior might affect others. For example, is a noisy game a good idea at 6.30 on a Sunday morning, when other people are probably trying to sleep? If you live in an apartment, should you practice your tap dancing at 10.00 on Tuesday night? Probably not!

Index

Picture Credits

(abbreviations: t = top; b = bottom;
m = middle; l = left; r = right)

THE AUTHOR

Paul Mason is a prolific author of children's books, many award-nominated, on such subjects as 101 ways to save the planet, vile things that go wrong with the human body, and the world's looniest inventors. Many take off via surprising, unbelievable, or just plain revolting facts. Today, he lives at a secret location on the coast of Europe, where his writing shack usually smells of a drying wetsuit (he's a former international swimmer and a keen surfer).